ROYAL ARMOURIES

Published by Royal Armouries Museum, Armouries Drive,
Leeds LS10 1LT, United Kingdom

www.royalarmouries.org

Copyright © 2017 Trustees of the Royal Armouries

ISBN 978 0 94809 281 7

Text by Natasha Bennett, Mark Murray-Flutter, Karen Watts

Edited by Martyn Lawrence

Designed by Geraldine Mead

Photography by Gary Ombler, Rod Joyce

Printed in Great Britain by Gomer Press Ltd

10 9 8 7 6 5 4 3 2 1

A CIP record for this book is available from the British Library

# INTRODUCTION

From the earliest times, the finest craftsmen in the world created beautiful objects for their wealthiest patrons. Worn by kings and coveted by emperors, these items not only revealed their owners' power and influence but also their standing as great patrons of art and culture. I am delighted to introduce the first book in a new series by the Royal Armouries Museum that showcases items which have adorned the great palaces, tournament fields and parade grounds of history. These are objects made to kill but also to impress: a magnificent testament to craftsmanship, engineering and high fashion.

**Dangerous Arts**

War is a universal phenomenon, its history dominated by a perpetual struggle for mastery. Arms and armour, however, give their own account of conflict. Sometimes derided as being inferior to paintings, sculpture and furnishings, in truth these objects tell stories like no others. Whether diplomatic gifts, rewards for services rendered, symbols of civic duty or icons of personal pride, many societies – Ottoman Turkey, Indo-Persia and Japan, amongst others – developed their own style of armour and weapons that shed light on cultural and technological advancement the world over.

*Dangerous Arts* presents some of the most stunning and decorative items in the Royal Armouries collection. Spanning more than half a millennium, the impact of the armour and weapons featured in this book resonate through history. They are witnesses to our shared past, speaking of the complex relationship between war, leadership and prowess in arms, as well as the reality (and fragility) of political, military and economic power. Among the most striking examples of practical and ceremonial art objects in the world, they convey profound messages about wealth, power, faith and loyalty. Here you will find armour from the royal courts of England, Saxony, the Venetian Republic and Japan; swords presented for distinguished service at Trafalgar and in the Crimean War; firearms used for hunting in imperial forests; and helmets from the high mountains of Persia.

## Protection and display

From the late middle ages to the early modern period a suit of armour protected the vulnerable human body during combat. Armourers first developed tight, overlapping joints that replaced vulnerable straps, and by 1400 full suits of plate armour were in existence. A carapace of overlapping and underlapping lames allowed limbs to bend and extend without revealing chinks in the armour. The fifteenth and sixteenth centuries marked the apogee of European plate armour: the degree of skill evinced in its design and fabrication is extraordinary, and several examples are offered here.

Eradicating chinks in the plate, however, was but one aim of the master armourer. In the upper reaches of his profession, high-end design was distinguished from the mundane by the beauty of the decoration and the quality of the materials. For the real artisan, unfettered by cost, imagination was the only limit. The resulting armour was worn on ceremonial occasions such as victory parades, state coronations and court events. The aura of authority that such armour projected on these occasions ultimately derived from its military, chivalric and heroic associations. It is revealing that monarchs and generals continued to wear suits of armour – in portraits, at least – as a badge of command long after their armies had abandoned them. Those who wore or displayed them intended to impress, to intimidate, and to communicate a message of untrammelled power.

Without exception, the armour and weapons featured in this book are both innovative and functional. They have been chosen as much for their style and status as for the practical purpose with which they are associated.

Many objects share a documented association with particular makers: here you will find the work of Tacca and Tiffany, Lorenzoni and Negroli. For centuries, only a few master craftsmen and workshops could create such products, and only the uppermost echelon of society could afford them. In their form, design and ornamentation, these objects rival in artistic value the great paintings and sculptural masterpieces of their time. The decoration on a piece of armour or a weapon not only distinguished a king from a commoner or a queen from a lady-in-waiting, but also revealed whether they were a genuine connoisseur of art and design or merely a blusterer who lacked the sophistication to patronise the finest craftsmen. This is a book that rewards close attention: in highlighting the detail, the artistry is elevated.

Cost was, of course, but one facet of an item's appeal. Its actual survival, often over many years, is also worthy of note. Collectors often prioritised specific designs, often with arcane imagery, that attested to their cultural and intellectual refinement. They invoke the *Schatzkammer* (treasure room) tradition, where valuable collections, often featuring precious metals or jewels, were kept in a secure chamber. Limited to those who could afford to create and maintain them, they became examples of private propaganda, places of discernment that transcended the reality outside. Items within them were social devices to establish and uphold one's rank in society. Their iconographic messages varied from Christian to chivalric to classical-mythological to Greco-Roman-Imperial, often harnessed in the service of dynastic propaganda. In such items – and, by extension, in the collector – the notion of legitimacy was writ large.

## Techniques and colouring

Techniques of decoration were perfected during the sixteenth century to embellish the white polished steel, wood, copper alloys and leather of traditional styles. These included embossing, gilding, damascening, etching, engraving, chiselling and casting. Blueing was also used as an adjunct to gilt surface decoration. Through this method, the steel was heated and, as it passed through a spectrum of colours, was arrested at an iridescent peacock blue. The Lion Armour featured here (pp. 39-43) was originally blue: although it has now oxidised to brown, little imagination is required to envisage this jaw-dropping piece of Italian Renaissance armour in its former glory.

A variety of colours could also be achieved by incrustations of gold, silver and precious stones. Painted decoration was used for parade and tournament, coordinating with rich textile fabrics worn by man and horse. The blades of swords could bear dedicatory inscriptions and makers' marks, and whilst the hilts bore the greatest variety of decoration, leather scabbards could also be faced with rich textiles and gilt metal finials. The locks, stocks and the barrels of firearms bore lavish forms of decoration on their steel and wood elements, as exemplified in these pages by the Tiffany revolver (pp. 48-9) and an astonishing platinum-plated, diamond-encrusted modern pistol (pp. 56-9).

These objects reflect changing fashions over the centuries, just as they show changing techniques of warfare, and occur across a wide geographical area. Such cultural distinctions of time and place are significant in the present too, as our own sensibilities respond to the decoration of the past. To the modern eye, developed in an era where modernism and minimalism have exerted a powerful influence, many of the most decorated objects can appear excessive, with surfaces filled to bursting point with engraving and gilding or inlays of coral, precious metals, bone and exotic woods. These embellishments reached a climax in the great international exhibitions of the nineteenth century, after which there began to emerge 'timeless classics', which relied for their effect on refined proportions, excellence of materials and superb craftsmanship.

**Karen Watts,**
Senior Curator of Armour and Art

# POWER, POMP AND PRIVILEGE

ARMS AND ARMOUR WERE PERFECT VEHICLES TO DEMONSTRATE ONE'S EXALTED POSITION IN SOCIETY. WHETHER ON PARADE OR CAMPAIGN, OUT HUNTING OR AT TOURNAMENTS, THE STAGE WAS SET TO 'DRESS TO IMPRESS' THROUGH THE ARMOUR WORN AND WEAPONS CARRIED.

# THE SOUTHAMPTON
# ARMOUR

*Probably French, about 1600*
*II.360*

This three-quarter armour is an outstanding example of late Mannerist decoration. Its etched and gilt overall pattern includes interlacing eared snakes in vertical bands, joined by foliage. This is inhabited by predatory birds, flying parrots, long-eared squirrels, hares, grasshoppers, dragonflies and snails (some winged).

This 'demilance' armour for the battlefield belonged to Henry Wriothesley, third earl of Southampton (1573-1624), the only patron acknowledged by Shakespeare. Both the shape and decoration of this armour illustrate the lengths and expense to which noblemen went in order to stand out before Queen Elizabeth.

Imprisoned in the Tower of London in 1601 for supporting Essex's rebellion against Elizabeth I, Southampton was released by King James I in 1603. Southampton later supported American settlement by the Virginia Company. He died while commanding English troops supporting the Dutch.

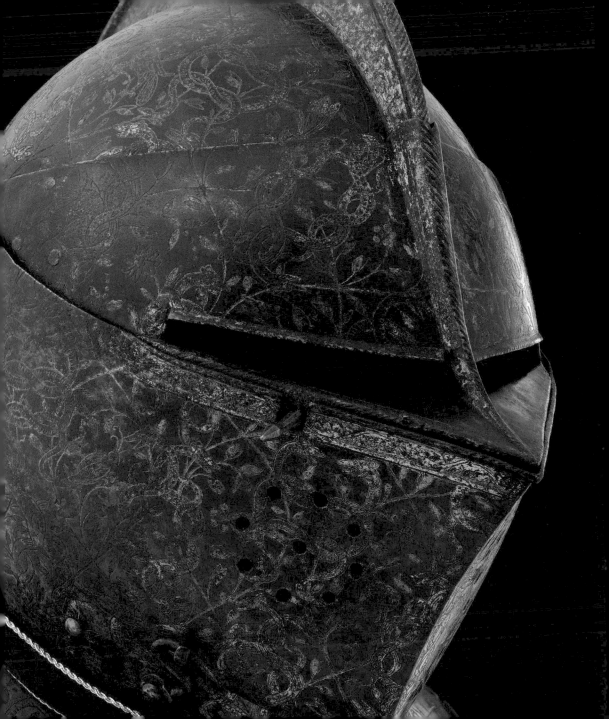

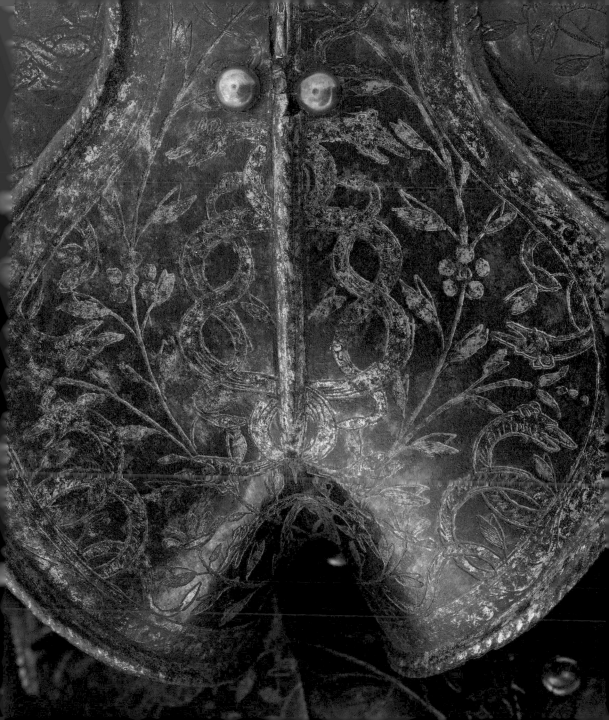

# POWDER FLASK

*Italian, late 16th century*
XIII.10

Throughout the late 16th and early 17th centuries powder flasks like these were used to recharge firearms – plain ones for ordinary soldiers and exquisitely-decorated ones for kings, princes and nobles and their ceremonial guards. From its sumptuous decoration we know that this object was almost certainly made for an important member of the Medici, Grand Dukes of Tuscany. Its decoration includes the arms of the family.

The body of the flask is of wood covered with rich red velvet, on top of which is laid a steel plate pierced, embossed and chiselled with ornament. The main feature of the design is Delilah, with the sleeping Samson in her arms, having just cut off his hair.

When this flask was made guns were far from common, and highly decorated ones were expensive items beyond the purse of all but the wealthiest gentlemen. Their level of decoration was a reflection of their owner's status.

# THE SMYTHE ARMOUR

*German, Augsburg, and English,*
*Royal Workshops at Greenwich, about 1585*
II.84, III.1430-1, VI.51, VI.115-6

Sir John Smythe was a soldier, military author and diplomat who served across Europe. In 1576, he was chosen as Queen Elizabeth I's special ambassador to Spain and was knighted by the queen. He wrote an important book that contributed to the debate on the merits of the bow over the gun.

This armour has many interchangeable pieces, and in the Royal Armouries collection are mounted as two armours. Both are light field (war) armours for fighting on foot and on horseback. The etched ornament includes a cross supported by angels and the heads of Janus, Minerva, Justice and other symbolic figures.

In 1596 Old Sir John Smythe was imprisoned in the Tower of London for uttering 'very seditious wordes'. Curiously in 1607 he bequeathed this armour to the monarch James I and thus it came to the Tower.

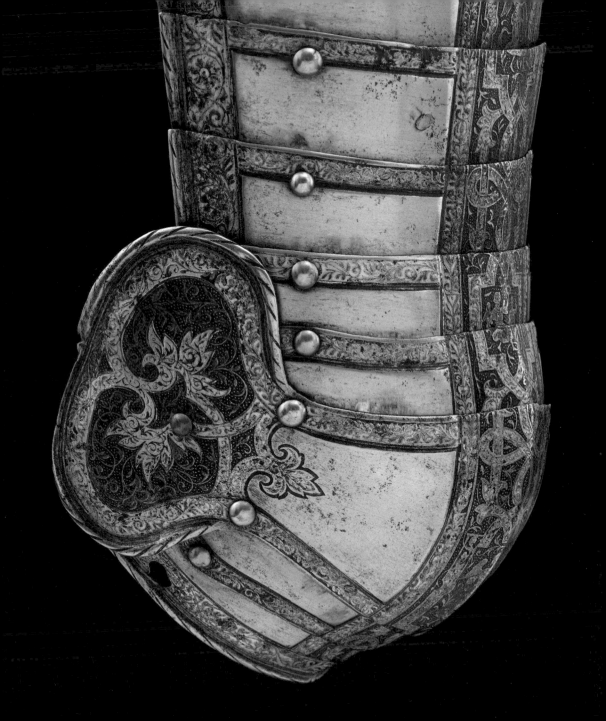

# IMPERIAL RUSSIAN
# SPORTING GUN

*Russian, Tula, 1752*
*XII.1504, XII.150*

Some wealthy women owned fine guns and enjoyed shooting. This elegantly decorated weapon belonged to Empress Elizabeth Petrovna, daughter of Peter the Great and Catherine I of Russia. In 1741 Elizabeth led a military coup and declared herself Empress of Russia. During her reign she encouraged the Russian arts, founding the Academy of Fine Arts in St Petersburg and the University of Moscow.

This flintlock gun was made at the Imperial Arms Workshop at Tula and bears her monogram. The stock is inlaid with silver wire with scrollwork and silver plates cut out and engraved with trophies of arms, classical figures and hunting scenes, in the French style. This forms part of a complete hunting set comprising the flintlock gun, a pair of pistols, a powder flask, a patch box and a pair of stirrups.

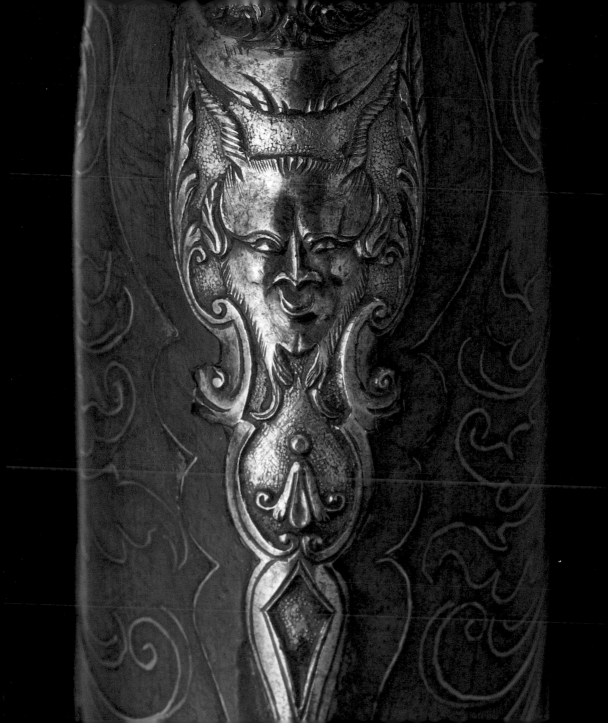

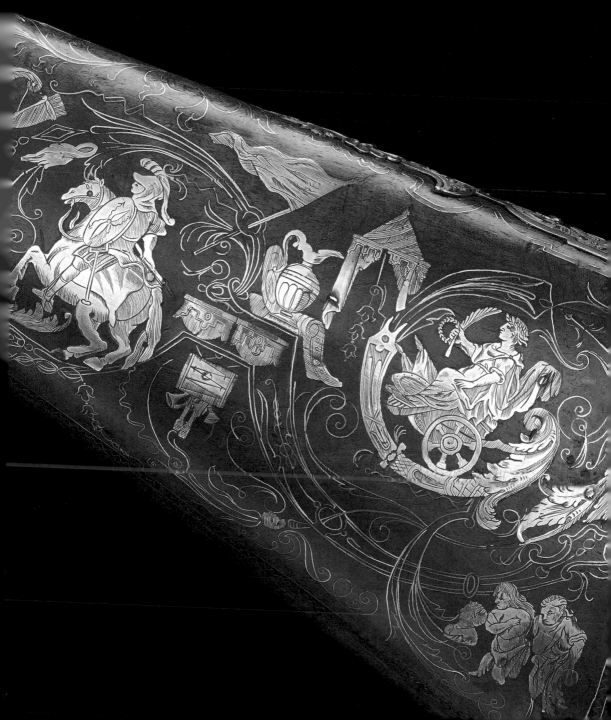

# SALLET

*German, 1490*

*IV.12*

It is rare for painted decoration on helmets to survive. Here, the upper part bears a flame pattern, whilst the lower part and the visor are painted with a chequered design in red, white and green. The squares are charged with stars, interlace and portcullises that simulate heraldic designs.

This versatile helmet of German origin is distinguished by a flattened crown and sweeping tail and visor. The visor is pierced with double sights: when lowered, this was ideal for use on horseback against a lance, whilst it could also be raised for all-round vision when fighting on foot. The long tail protected the nape of the neck, allowing the head to tilt back to face a cavalryman. The helmet had an internal lining and chin-straps, and may also have had a decorative textile covering which would have been laced via the pairs of small rivet holes.

# THE CAPODILISTA ARMOUR

*Italian, about 1620*

II.192

This steel suit of armour mimics a textile suit of fashionable clothes. It is etched with a repeat pattern, imitating a woven textile cloth, probably custom-made. Each arch contains a double-headed eagle under a crown. This is the device of count Annibale Capodilista, a noble from Padua, Italy.

The family was given their title and the right to display the Imperial Eagle by the Holy Roman Emperor. Count Annibale had a strong military career as a condottiere (mercenary captain) in the service of the Venetian Republic. Although a fashion statement, this armour was still a functioning cuirassier field armour for war.

Another classic element of fashion is the wearing of jewellery. The armour has a representation of a gilt chain around the neck with a medallion of the Crucifixion with the Virgin Mary and St John the Evangelist. The skull and crossbones signify Mount Calvary from the Latin 'calvaria', skull.

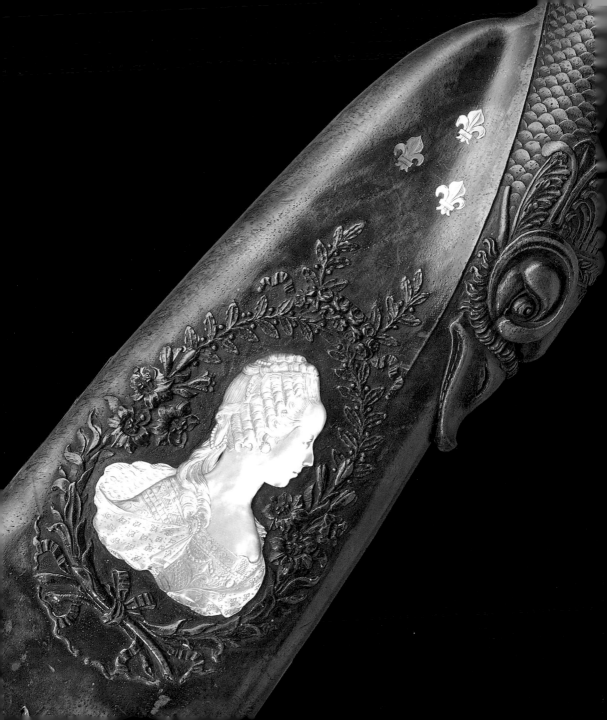

# CROSSBOW

*French, mid 18th century*
XI.93

This magnificent crossbow was traditionally the property of Queen Marie Leczinska (1703-68), daughter of Stanisław I of Poland and consort of Louis XV of France. Such bows were usually intended for small birds and game. Made by gun- and crossbow-maker Christian Trincks (active between 1714 and 1732) in Strasburg, the forepart of the steel is intricately chiselled with foliage involving monsters, figures and grotesque masks, with birds fluttering against a gilt background.

The walnut stock is reminiscent of a later style of French stock. Inlaid on the right-hand side is a portrait bust, likely of Marie Antoinette (and thus probably applied later), with three fleur-de-lys all in mother of pearl. Inlaid on the left-hand side is a silver figure of Diana, worshipped by the Romans as goddess of the hunt and by the Greeks as goddess of fertility. The portrayal of Diana may be significant in light of the crossbow's female ownership: in 1575, the French ambassador reported that Elizabeth I was also an expert huntswomen with a light bow.

# ARTISTS, DESIGNERS AND CRAFTSMEN

THE MAKING OF SUPERB ARMOURS AND WEAPONS FREQUENTLY INVOLVED MANY SKILLED CONTRIBUTORS. SOMETIMES WE NO LONGER KNOW THE IDENTITIES OF THE MASTER CRAFTSMEN INVOLVED. HOWEVER, HERE WE CAN SEE THE REMARKABLE INFLUENCES OF ARTISTS LIKE GIAMBOLOGNA, DESIGNERS LIKE CLAUDE SIMONIN AND MASTER CRAFTSMEN SUCH AS FILIPPO NEGROLI.

# THE LION ARMOUR

*Probably Italian, about 1550*
II.89

This is one of the finest examples of Italian Renaissance embossed armour. All available curved surfaces are decorated with lions' heads, framed by flowing manes, with jaws open to bare their teeth. The remaining surfaces were then blued (now naturally oxidised to brown) alternating with panels of exceptionally fine decoration in false gold damascening.

This armour must have been created for a splendid heroic lion-themed court tournament event. Significantly, this armour came to the British Royal Armouries from the French Royal Armouries, now called the Musée de l'Armée, Paris where another lion-themed armour is known. This suggests that the Lion Armour was made for a royal prince of France.

It was designed to be used not only on horseback with lance and sword but also on foot. Despite it being a sculptural work of art, it could still save the wearer's life in combat. Indeed, this armour clearly has done so: the helmet has distinct sword-cuts.

# HORSE'S HEAD DEFENCE
# (SHAFFRON)

*Italian, about 1590*

VI.52

In an era when men fought, jousted and travelled on horseback, ownership of fine horses demonstrated prestige and power. Horses were not only equipped with armour for war but also for ceremonial parades and tournaments. This shaffron is part of a matching set for both the horse and the rider. It protected the upper part of the horse's head with shaped and flanged defences for the ears and eyes.

Despite the ornate decoration, it is a fully functioning piece of armour that will deflect blows. In the centre is a later twisted fluted spike, that gives it a mystical unicorn appearance. The background is finely matted with a punch and was probably blued or blackened. The surface comprises engraved and gilt cartouches with scrolled ends set diagonally and containing floral ornament. Set at intervals are stars, embossed and originally silvered.

# THE ZAOUE FLINTLOCK
# SPORTING GUN

*French, about 1853*
*XII.5696*

This double-barrelled flintlock sporting gun was made by Zaoue, a gunmaker in Marseille, southern France. The barrels are engraved with 'canons de Leclerc', made by Joseph Leclerc of St Remy, Liege, Belgium. They are stamped with Liege proofmarks. This demonstrates that however beautiful this gun may be as a work of art, it is also a fully-functioning hunting firearm.

The stock, locks and breeches are all decorated with inlaid vines and bunches of grapes. The vine tendrils are engraved into the stock connecting the vine leaves. The entire gun is decorated ensuite with matching engraved inlays accentuated by a colour opposition of gold and silver leaves.

# THE TIFFANY
# REVOLVER

*American, 1989*
XII.9609

This Smith & Wesson model 29 .44 Magnum revolver was commissioned by the Royal Armouries in 1990 from Tiffany & Co. of New York and took more than 400 hours of craftsmanship to complete.

The decorative scheme developed by Tiffany's designers was based on the leaves and branches of five species of tree whose wood had been used in the manufacture of English weapons. The cast grip and the cylinder are carpeted by four different types of leaves (oak, ash, elm and walnut), each individually plated in different shades of 22-carat gold.

Oak, ash, walnut and elm were chosen to represent indigenous English trees traditionally associated with the crafting of firearms, oak and ash having been used in the making of gun carriages. The barrel and frame is inlaid with representations of the branches and fruit of the yew tree, used to manufacture the longbow that was so instrumental in the English victories of the Hundred Years War.

# THE LORENZONI
# FLINTLOCK GUN

*Italian, about 1695*

XII.1692

Michele Lorenzoni is recorded as working in Florence around 1685. The barrel of this gun is by the Spanish gunmaker Nicolas Bis. Michele Lorenzoni's guns are not only famous for their technical expertise, but also for their chiselled decoration. This gun has particularly rare and exquisite silver mounts that show numerous human figures in conflict. A particularly fine panel shows a cascading trophy of arms in the classical manner.

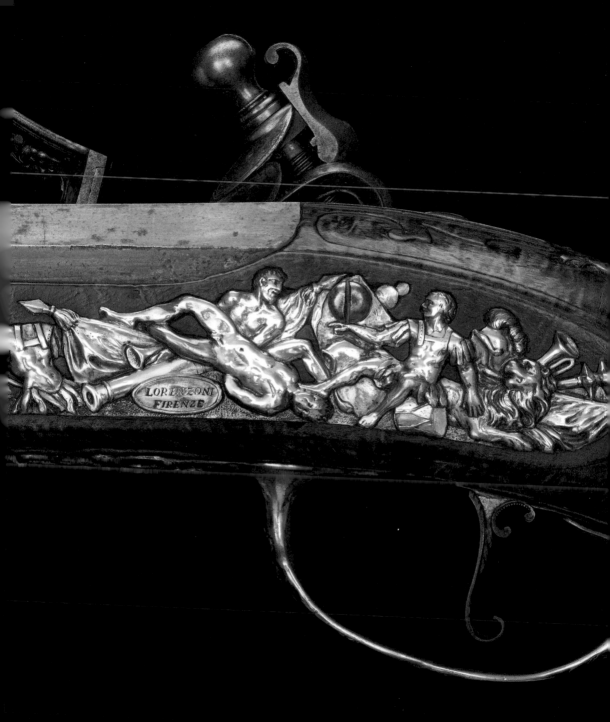

# THE TACCA
# SWORD HILT

*Italian, Florence, about 1640*

IX.2156

P ietro Tacca was a Florentine sculptor and the chief pupil of Giambologna. After his master's death, Tacca completed a number of his works and succeeded him as sculptor to the Medici Grand Dukes of Tuscany. He also created an equestrian statue in 1640 of King Philip IV of Spain who, by his own wish, is shown on a rearing horse. This was an unprecedented technical feat of bronze casting on this scale and Tacca had scientific advice from Galileo.

This sword hilt may have been made either for a similar sculpture or to be carried as part of a formal parade dress sword. It is not completely pierced through the attachment of the blade. It is cast in one piece in bronze and represents the head of an oriental male emerging from a hooded jacket. Beneath are Mannerist distorted masks. The guard is shaped as animal legs with cloven hooves.

# CENTREFIRE
# SIX-SHOT REVOLVER

*American, 1996*

XII.11824

O ne of the most ornate and flamboyant firearms in the Royal Armouries collection is this
diamond-encrusted .357 Smith & Wesson. It was
designed and created in 1996 by Sussex goldsmith
Edward Evans, who has produced a variety of
highly-decorated firearms for clients that include
the famous London jewellers Asprey and Garrard.

The base revolver is a Smith & Wesson Model 60
made in stainless steel. It has been highly polished
and finished in engine-turned guilloche to produce
an intricate geometric pattern. Platinum and
white 18-carat gold finishes and castings are also
applied to the surface, inset into which are more
than 900 brilliant-cut Sierra Leone diamonds.
The grip is decorated with guilloche and covered
in a deep, lustrous blue enamel. On completion
of the work, thirty rounds were fired to confirm
that the applied decoration would remain stable.

This pistol was a victim of the 1997 Firearms
Amendment Act, and was surrendered to Sussex
police for a compensation payment of £65,000.

# GIFTS, GOODWILL AND GRATITUDE

WHETHER COMMISSIONED
FOR AN OFFICIAL
PRESENTATION OR
TO BE GIVEN AS AN INDIVIDUAL
EXPRESSION OF FRIENDSHIP
OR ESTEEM, THESE FINE
OBJECTS COULD BE UNIQUELY
PERSONAL STATEMENTS.
FROM THE DIPLOMATIC GIFT
TO THE WEDDING PRESENT,
IT WAS 'THE THOUGHT
THAT COUNTS'.

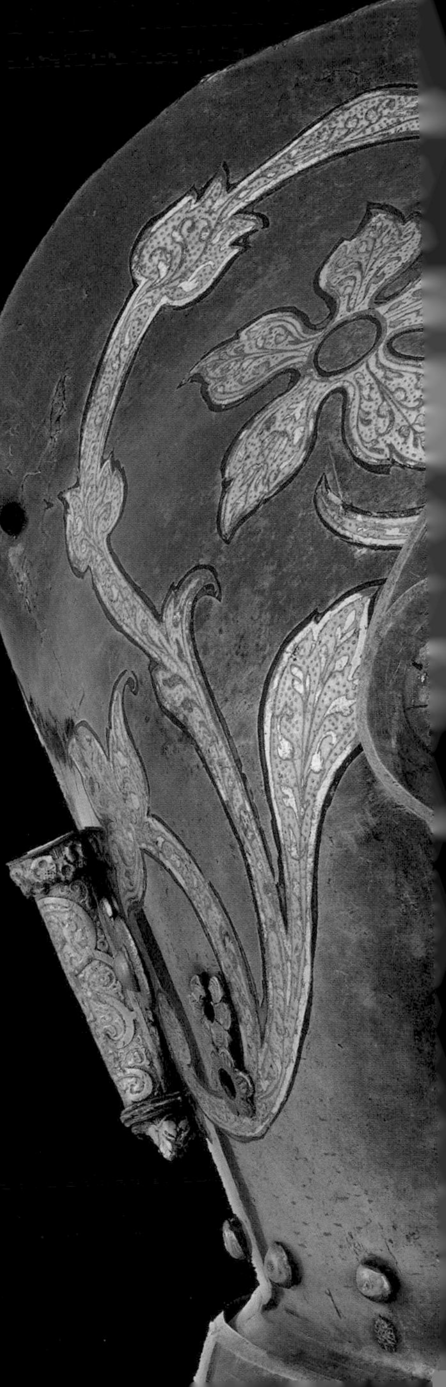

# FOOT TOURNEY
# ARMOUR

*German, Augsburg, 1591*

II.186

In 1591 Sophia of Brandenburg ordered this and a set of eleven identical armours as a Christmas present for her husband, Christian I, Elector of Saxony. The armours were made by Anton Peffen-hauser of Augsburg (1525–1603), the foremost German armourer of his day, and were decorated with etching and gilding with bold floral scrolls. This armour retains its original blued finish, as well as rare examples of linings in the helmet and gauntlets.

They were made as half armours for wear in the foot tournament with pikes over the barriers. Sadly Christian died in September 1591 before the armours were delivered. Sword cuts on the close helmet show that the armour was actually used in the tournament. The group of armours is now divided between collections in St Petersburg, Crakow, Dresden, Nuremberg, London, New York and Detroit.

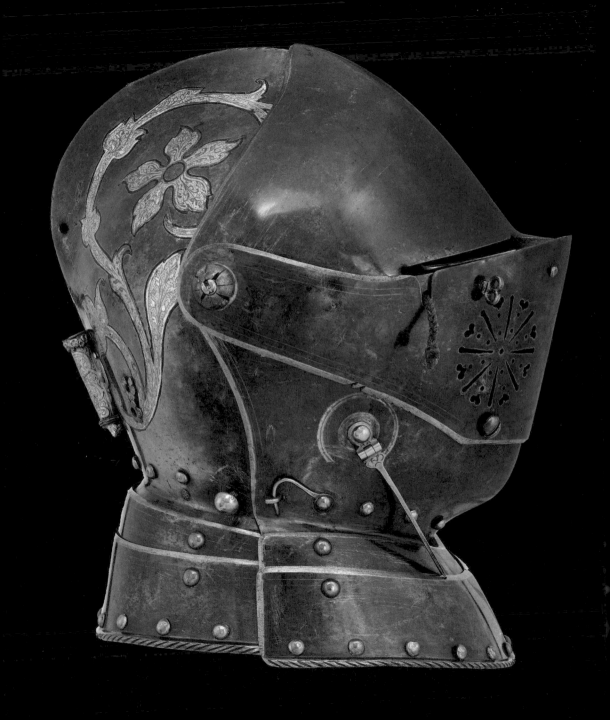

# THE FENWICK
# WILLIAMS SWORD

*English, London, 1856*

*IX.1841*

The Legislature of Nova Scotia commissioned this remarkable sword for presentation to Sir William Fenwick Williams (1800-83) who was born at Annapolis, Nova Scotia. The hilt and scabbard are of silver, parcel gilt, and are of remarkable quality. They were made by the great artist-craftsman Antoine Vechte, 'the Cellini of the 19th century', who at this time had moved from Paris to work for the London silversmiths Hunt and Roskell.

The presentation recognised Sir William's command during the Crimean War of the forces defending the Turkish town of Kars against overwhelming Russian forces. After capitulation in 1855 in the face of impossible odds and captivity in Russia, Sir William returned and was created a baronet and a Knight Commander of the Order of the Bath. The sword's decoration uniquely reflects Williams' origins, service and achievements and includes the seal of Nova Scotia, a bear and a camel.

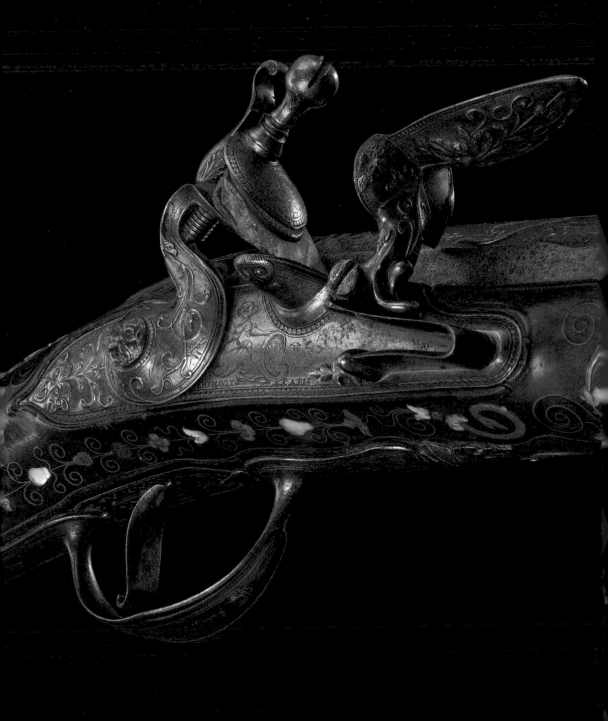

# THE BERTHAULT FLINTLOCK SPORTING GUN

*French, about 1670*
*XII.10479*

This sporting flintlock gun appears to have been a sumptuous wedding gift and an example of French international intrigue.

In 1674, Philip Herbert, 7th earl of Pembroke, married Henriette de Kérouaille. It is interesting to note that this gun was given by the diplomat Charles Colbert, marquis de Croissy, who was the French ambassador to London at the court of King Charles II. Colbert had gained the king's favour by finding him a mistress, Louise de Kérouaille, sister of the bride. Colbert seems to have given his own precious gun made by Antoine Berthault, a noted French gunmaker.

The arms of Charles Colbert are on the escutcheon plate and the arms of France are on the lockplate. The barrel is damascened in gold. The lock is chiselled and engraved and the stock is profusely inlaid in silver with scrollwork and foliage involving animals, birds and various emblems.

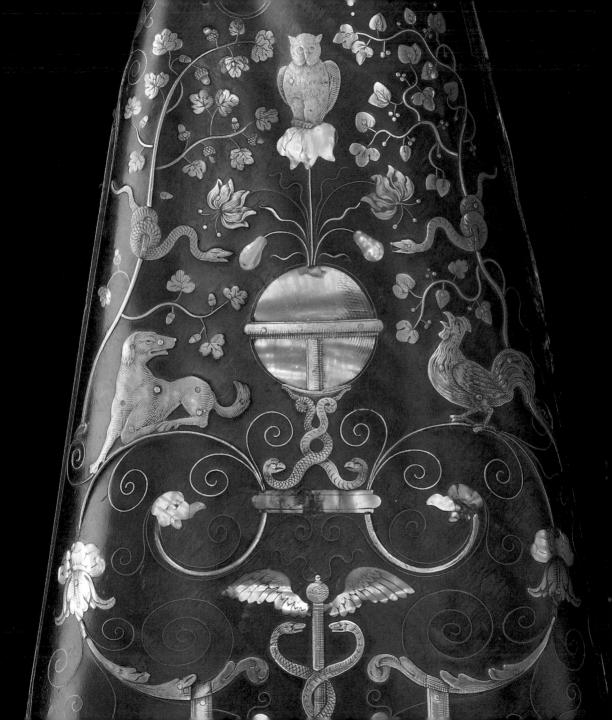

# 'THE BURGUNDIAN BARD'

*Flanders, about 1511-14*
VI. 6-12

This stunning horse armour was a gift from the Holy Roman Emperor Maximilian I to King Henry VIII of England, presented to mark the latter's marriage to Katherine of Aragon in 1509. It is embossed with a trailing design of pomegranates (Katherine of Aragon's badge) and the firesteels and ragged crosses of the Burgundian Order of the Golden Fleece (with which Henry had been awarded in 1505).

The armourer was Guillem Margot, who worked in the Emperor's Flemish territories. The decorator responsible for the fine engraving was Paul van Vrelant, who is first recorded working in Brussels for the Imperial family.

The 'bard' was originally even more magnificent: although little remains today, the whole of the exterior was originally silvered and at least partly gilded. Henry VIII was clearly impressed with the decoration since he soon persuaded van Vrelant to come to England, employing him as 'the king's harness gilder' from 1514.

# THE ADMIRAL LORD
# COLLINGWOOD SWORD

*English, London, 1806-7*

IX.909

This sword celebrates victory at the naval battle of Trafalgar. It was made to the order of the Corporation of the City of London for pre-sentation to Cuthbert, Admiral Lord Collingwood to express its gratitude following his action in taking command of the British fleet at Trafalgar in 1805 after the mortal wounding of Admiral Lord Horatio Nelson.

The sword was supplied by Thomas Harper, a goldsmith who had formerly been in business in Charlestown, North Carolina, and the Dutch East Indies before setting up in London in 1783. The hilt is of solid gold set with enamel plaques bearing the arms of the City of London and of Collingwood. The knuckle-guard is enamelled in blue and set in diamonds on one side spelling out 'TRAFALGAR' and on the other the famous order issued by Nelson 'ENGLAND EXPECTS EVERY MAN TO DO HIS DUTY'.

# THE 'FORGET-ME-NOT' GUN

*French, about 1585*
XII.1764

This 16th-century wheellock pistol confounds expectations: it is a gun, but it is also a work of art and more than that, it is a gift of love. Although a stunning work of art in its own right, the associated mystery surrounding the giver and receiver of this intensely passionate gift is what makes it a particularly fascinating piece.

Amid the decoration are several amazing images, including two painted miniatures of a bearded man and an erotic figure of a woman in a suggestive pose. An actual flower, pressed and gilt in a glass medallion, has a German inscription *Ver Gis Mein Nit*, 'Forget Me Not', to make the message clear.

As a work of art it demonstrates a rare combination of decorative techniques such as chiselling, inlaid gold and silver, miniature painting and the rare verre églomisé technique (glass gilded with gold-leaf and painted on the reverse).

# CONFLICT, COMMERCE AND CULTURE

INE ARMS AND ARMOUR HAVE BEEN PRODUCED IN ALMOST EVERY CULTURE WORLDWIDE. AS EUROPEAN EMPIRES DEVELOPED, WARS, DIPLOMACY AND TRADE STIMULATED CROSS-CULTURAL INFLUENCES AND THE TASTE FOR THE EXOTIC. PIECES FROM AFRICA, ASIA AND OTHER FAR-FLUNG LOCATIONS WERE IMPORTED, INSPIRING NEW FASHIONS, NOT LEAST IN ARMS AND ARMOUR.

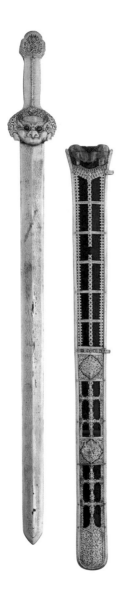

# CHINESE MING DYNASTY SWORD

*Chinese, early 15th century*
XXVIS.295

Tibetan Buddhism was introduced into China in the Yuan and the early years of the Ming dynasties. This sword was probably made for imperial presentation to one of the great Tibetan monasteries.

The hilt is of gilt iron with a wooden core and the grip is punched with small circles to imitate fish skin. The guard is embossed in the form of a monster mask, surmounted by a silvered crescent and a golden disc. The face is textured with finely punched circles, the canine teeth chiselled and gilt. The horns are in the form of crab claws. The staring eyes were made of rock crystal over red foil. At either side of the mouth is a paw in the form of a human hand. The head is surrounded by scrolling curls of mane. The surreal monster mask is known in Tibetan as *chibar* – 'that which resembles nothing'.

# II ARMOUR

*Japanese, Momoyama and Edo period*

XXVIA.224

Ii Naomasa (1561–1602) was one of the four generals of Tokugawa Ieyasu, the eventual victor in the civil wars that overshadowed 16th-century Japan. He commanded a regiment of arquebusiers at the battle of Nagakute in 1584, and was fatally injured by a musket ball at the battle of Sekigahara in 1600. Naomasa adopted blood red lacquered armour, and his descendants' armours, which can be seen in Hikone Castle today, all followed the same pattern, including the tall horns covered in gold lacquer.

The helmet of this armour is of the simple five-plate type popularised by the armourer Hineno Hironari in the late 16th century, and is of the period of Naomasa himself, though his personal armour is thought to be one of the series preserved at Hikone. The remainder of this armour is laced in white, green and purple silk braid, contrasting dramatically with the red lacquer, and belonged to a later member of the family.

# 'TURBAN' HELMET

*Turkish, late 15th century*
XXVIA.142, 145

This helmet or *migfer* is etched and overlaid in silver and gold with Arabic calligraphy. The lower inscription lists the titles of the unnamed Sultan whom the owner of the helmet served, 'glorifier of the faith, victorious, triumphant king, to him be lasting prosperity, wealth, power, peace and health'. The upper inscription is a line from a poem popular on medieval metalwork in Persia, 'to its owner good fortune, peace and health throughout his lifetime, as long as the doves coo'.

Though the Sultan is unnamed, it is most probably the Ak-Koyonlu (White Sheep Turcoman) sultan Ya'qub (1478–90). It is likely that this helmet was a trophy of the great victory of the Ottoman Sultan Selim the Grim over the Safavids at the battle of Çaldiran in 1514. Helmets of this type exemplify some of the most beautiful examples of the Islamic armourer's craft.

# MIQUELET RIFLE

*Turkish, 19th century*
XXVIF.6

F irearms were very important in the Turkish army from the middle of the 16th century, and the characteristic weapons of the elite infantry corps, the Janissaries. In the 18th century they replaced their old matchlock weapons with a distinctive type of flintlock used across the Ottoman Empire, called *cakmakli tufek* or *shishane*.

Though practical fighting weapons, they were often fitted like this one with rifled barrels of Damascus steel, and usually extravagantly decorated; this one has a hardwood stock heavily inlaid with panels of green-stained and natural walrus ivory and dark horn, and ornamented with millefiori patterns in brass wire, while the lock and barrel are heavily overlaid with floral scrolls in silver.

# HELMET

*Indian, late 18th century*
XXVIA.12

This Indian helmet is a thoroughly intriguing object. The piece is highly decorative, with much of the helmet bowl covered in shining details picked out in *koftgari* (a technique involving the overlay of gold and silver on iron and steel).

Like similar items produced during the late 18th and early 19th centuries, this helmet was probably used for public ceremonies, parades or display. The fragility of the mail aventail supports this theory: whilst the tiny butted links are woven into a strikingly-patterned veil, they would have provided little protection in combat.

The repeated motif of a skull over crossed bones makes the helmet very distinctive. Geometric and floral patterns were common choices in the subcontinent, whereas these skull designs (implying the inevitability of mortality) appear to be more European in nature. Possibly a local patron wished to integrate Western inspiration in his armour, or signify membership of a group whose identity is now a mystery.